Trieste
Nichola Deane

smith|doorstop

Published 2015 by
smith|doorstop Books
The Poetry Business
Bank Street Arts
32-40 Bank Street
Sheffield S1 2DS

Copyright © Nichola Deane 2015
All Rights Reserved

ISBN 978-1-910367-44-5
Typeset by Utter
Printed by MPG Biddles

Acknowledgements
I'd like to thank the magazines in which early drafts of some of these poems appeared: *The Moth*, *The SHOp*, *Oxford Poetry*, *The Interpreter's House*, *The North* and *The Rialto*. 'Jude's Rain' appears in the *Crystal Voices Anthology* (2015).

smith|doorstop Books are a member of Inpress:
www.inpressbooks.co.uk. Distributed by Central Books Ltd.,
99 Wallis Road, London E9 5LN

The Poetry Business gratefully acknowledges the support
of Arts Council England.

Contents

5	Bowl
6	Portrait of Georg Trakl
7	Three Shades of Black
8	New York in the Poet
9	L'Estartit
10	November, December
11	'What Can a Flame Remember?'
12	November, December II
13	Yesterday's Child
14	Behave, Moriarty
16	The Sex Life of Bedbugs
17	Fig Ghazal
18	Thanked Be Fortune
19	A Stocking Mask for Pussy Riot
20	Standing Poem for Erdem Gunduz
21	Ode to Concentration
22	Jude's Rain
23	Coming out of the lake into a big towel and her arms
24	Raasay, Hallaig and After
25	Quinto Del Sordo
27	Cityscape with Invisible Dog
28	The Song of the Three Flames
29	Cap Stone
30	To the Reader
31	Trieste

for my parents

Bowl

> *Drink and be whole again beyond confusion.*
> – Robert Frost

Or wood or bone or mud or plastic or silver,
with a family tree as long as history,
what are you, split-skull? What don't you know?
If we've forged an axe, we've dreamed a bowl,
if we've made a fire we've made you a home
for food, for bread (a womb for bread) for wine
and water and milk-into-wine. But what are you for
if not for everything? O room for absence

open to the sky! A home but not a roof.
We might say: a love without its shelter.
You place no seal on your pure hollow of praise –
praising's tomb. And if dust touches you
it sleeps in an eyelid bed, in half a world
singing lullay: *be here be whole be gone.*

Portrait of Georg Trakl
after a drypoint by Milein Cosman

I have closed your book long since
but you're still staring your howl at me
from the locked ward of its pages.

Your eyes will not be walled up in that white.

The marks on that sketch are blurred in
left to right, as if, bridling, you'd just
jerked your head, mid-glare.

Under the recess of your brows is a long drop.

And I think of the one my father told me of,
the time he'd lain at the lip of the flooded quarry
and lowered the longest line he could

– butcher's string or a ball of twine –

weighted at the end with a stone adze
into the black water. Down it dropped
and down until he held the string by its tip

as it shuddered in the depths like a distressed pendulum.

Three Shades of Black

Here! clothe yourself completely in swathes
of Lorca black, better to absorb the noonday sun.
Or strip to enter this flinty Dunkeld

burn, troubled with its own brightness,
weaving and wilding its black snow-water,
yet beading clear on the swimmer's skin.

Either way you'll end as you must: *a-cold,
burning* – starless black, Rothko-black,
dense, mineral, on black ground.

New York in the Poet
after the Self Portrait 1929-31 by Federico García Lorca

My face contains
three moons or more
(black moons, black moons:
three small black moons).
A hand like smoke
combs out my dreams.

The moons are falling like rain, now,
in a year of lunar rain.

The roots of a tree
(or are they the roots of lightning?)
climb the skyscrapers
and brownstones behind me,
then leap from them
like elegant suicides
or circus artistes
dangling from invisible wire

while the moons continue falling
in a first-last rain

(little omegas
when they break on stone)
and the leaves in the park turn black
and twist and suck
and swell like leeches.

L'Estartit
my father in Catalonia, 1961

'Careful.' The barman jerked his head
a little towards the closing door,
thumping, as if punch-drunk, on its hinges.

'Careful, *senyor*. Special Police. *Guardia
Civil* –' and, stepping back from his gaze
again, carried on revolving and polishing,

revolving and polishing, with plain white
linen, a clean, warm brandy balloon
so that there would soon be

no hint of fingerprint (those telling
whorls and loops like Celtic beasts)
no cloudy planets of human grease

on its surface when he raised it,
a breathed-on, empty chalice, up
to the one small source of natural light.

November, December

November is eternal till it's gone.

No late glories or bare finalities,
just the throes of the leaves.

There and there and there, then not:
a long there, then a now.

There's always something less

November has to do, until
the month throws up its hands in gale and gust,

winter coming on like a scene change,
like the dropping into sense and half-coherence

of an unpainted blocked-out backdrop.

'What Can a Flame Remember?'
– Seferis

A flame remembers one near thing:
the heat rounding

on the spark,
the jolt of its beginning.

Not the world, nor the story,
nor the gospel of dark.

Nothing beyond the pale
of its own burning –

just the arc,
the ark of fire,

but not
the transitory,

the soul in fall

November, December II

i.

November's a wheezy sigh,
December an intake of breath.
One a chronic fatigue,
the other – a bastard faith.
Downcast – a *pendant shoot of ice*,
like Johnson says an icicle is,
a spike, a spine, a thorn of faith
gone to earth. A weeping,
see-through tongue.

ii.

Present dangers, both, these months lived
as if painful to the body,
as if interior, symptoms in the flesh.
Why is the waiting for leaf-fall no less of an ache
than the sight of the empty tree?
That the full moon looks cold and especially naked
this time of year.
That the immaculate blackbird nest is visible
within its spirit canopy.

Yesterday's Child

Sorrow and rage, rage and sorrow
are beads on a thread of ragged prayer

and yesterday's child can't cut the string
and her life is strung on thin thin air

she knowingly doggedly sowing tomorrow
with sorrow and rage and rage and sorrow

Behave, Moriarty

Take this!
Kneel, I command you.
There there.

I stopped. Did you
feel it stopping?
Did you breathe?

This is my fingers
drawing tighter.
This, your throat.

Whenever a word
reaches you it's iron,
forge-fired.

Damn you? I can.
I smell your skin –
singed, on fire.

Scars: yes yes.
Hole, ridge,
socket, blister.

The worst words
are those held back.
A key turns.

The same pain
replicated
is noise, no?

While the quality
of mercy is
silence, surcease.

You ... look ... anxious,
dear. Oh *dear*.
Do mop up.

A cloth?
Bleach. Better
neat. You've missed

a bit. Good
dog. Woof.
Kiss kiss.

The Sex Life of Bedbugs
for A.S.

Scientist, like a true artist, for three
years you fed the colony on your own blood,
syringing a supply from one arm or the other
daily, until they felt like progeny.
And how did they thank you? In the only way they knew:
they copulated magnificently and were fruitful,
multiplying in such numbers, enthusiasts
of the entombed peep show under glass
in microscopic slo-mo close-up.

So different from their normal assignations.
One imagines a *spiccato* one-two
of the hypodermic genitalia
on grubby postage-stamp sized sheets,
haemoglobin mojitos warming
nearby on a tray the size of a contact lens.
All around them, the scent of coriander
grows more lush with their arousal,
their lust, Roman, vast as the universe.

Fig Ghazal

I am ghazal.
I am ghazal in the way that split fig
is split fig, and ripeness ripeness,
ghazal in knowing no other.

All is ghazal
and for the women
in their world-purdah,
with their force, drift, thrift,
make-shine, ache-shift,
their time-signature, I sing it, this

my body, the poured-out song you hear
muffled on the other side of the locked door.

Thanked Be Fortune

this breath escapes
what mind cannot
to
              – changed air –

– charged sky –

A Stocking Mask for Pussy Riot

I'd pulled the nylon over until it was
near-stifling. No eye-holes till I poked
and tore them in. Before that I felt larval
or as though trapped in the birth canal.
Almost blind. My head squeezed on all sides
as if remembering the muscle that released me
once. So, with hair-scissors I cut my way
to a second sense of sight – and saw the I
inside me doing time, once such a model
prisoner. Eyes insurgent and incendiary.
How I've stared myself down all my life –
but –*Basta, Basta!* Oh yes, and I've more than
data on you, sonny boy. Don't think
you're getting away with any of this shit.

Standing Poem for Erdem Gunduz
Taksim Square, Istanbul, June 2013

Fellow-thinking is like the triangular, slight asymmetry you adopt,
gazing up at the face of the giant leader on his great stone wall.

Hands in your pockets, taking breath into blood,
you restrain nothing but the impulse to forbid.

Warmed by your flesh, questions assume the vitality of passions,
the velocity and sharpness of arrows waiting in their quiver.

Where you stand, you dance
an assembly of the deepest solitude.

A cornucopia of scrutiny, Erdem,
a legion of one.

Ode to Concentration

Thinking brimming into biding,
an entire staying
with some thing, making, idea,
companionably, unutterably,
– eye, mind, body,
heart –with or without fury or fear,
beyond end or ends,
as you might the path of a river
or the flight of a bird,
staying as long as sight permits, then longer,
staying beyond the brink of the seen
into day's fall and failure,
until you can no longer
sense the river in the ocean,
until the wing-shape is less
than a mote or a tremor,
has become, if only to you,
the blue into which it vanishes.

Jude's Rain

St Jude, the day after his storm, 29th October 2013

Even storms can become lost
and what threatens most lower its fist,
so how close to blest I am to watch
the rain shake all the light from the air

like my mother on the back step
with the white tablecloth:
the rain as it trembles once in fear,
then trembles into new meaning,

its falling held, and
                                      shaken sideways,
shaken clean.

Coming out of the lake into a big towel and her arms
after lines by Anne Carson

When the mother opens her arms to her child, the corners of the towel
in either hand, what is it that moves me further, deeper?
                                                        The thought of my running
to some such embrace, the great imprecise blur of running and memory,
(not a lake but a bay, day's end, and the warmth, the double warmth
of cloth and arms, her spilling smile and running that way to my mother –
to be her smile or that smile's excess –)

or
            the thought of either of my sons doing the same
                                              and that face that was hardly hers
coming into my face like a sunset, breaking my love right down to its colours,
my face dissolving, then, into the bass of all feeling,
night welling in my face, dissolving, reaching the root of every love?

Raasay, Hallaig and After

...the look of unmasked light.
      –Alice Oswald

You are flayed whiteness
of whittled silver birch-wood.

You are the roe bounding away
over bramble, moss and proud root.

And you are all my deranged
cogencies, sweet unasked

of-a-sudden unmaskings.
O stay and be to me the light

exactly, what it does.
Be to me still the unmasked light.

Quinto Del Sordo *
Goya at home, March 1819

These shutters banging tonight
in a dry wind (I don't get up to close them)

in a dry wind, impatient of night!
I stick out my tongue to taste the air

that tastes of dust, dust and elsewhere:
beyond despair, the sated nameless dust ...

What use, that taste of afterwards?
What comfort? When I can see the waking wind

but never hear it? What will I ever know
of the soul of this damned house?

(Though the flute of my bones has the wind's ear)
Does the frame of it groan in the wind's shift?

I wouldn't know what note lifts and falls. Only
that the looming voices and faces I see and hear

– inside? outside? – my mind, that roam these rooms,
are darkly clear, clouding near

like tarry smoke devilled with sulphur.
O paint our murmur, for your own sake! they beg me nightly,

*paint our blur, which is the pain before the rendering,
before the laying-in and dust!*

Somehow the night must grow a hand.
Somehow the cackle grows a tooth.

They gape and grab while the pale walls wait for me,
whimper their blankness, sad as dogs.

*'House of the Deaf Man,' located on the outskirts of Madrid, where Goya, by then deaf, lived between February 1819-1823, and where he painted, on the walls, his celebrated 'Black Paintings,' since removed to the Prado. The house had already acquired the name 'Quinto Del Sordo' when Goya bought it: the previous occupant was also deaf. It was demolished in 1909.

Cityscape with Invisible Dog
after a remark by Donald Justice

My dog is in the poem though he isn't mentioned.
He trails along behind me in my sadness,
his leash not quite at full stretch, working
his nose up and down the regularly spaced
lampposts, squeezing his nostrils like a concertina.
You will not hear these inhalations in the poem:
the dog is in the rain but a different rain
which soaks him but is otherwise no tribulation.
Rain he does not howl at or invest with feeling
and when he lifts his leg in graceful attitude
it is to make a delible stink in the world.

The Song of the Three Flames

Bide, though the sum
of your life is like camphor,

whose blue fume is the scent
of a truant god.

Bide your time,
though the smile of it is like tallow,

whose flame came of flesh
and the squeal of death.

Bide here, now, for now,
though the work of it is a flame like beeswax:

a shine made of infinite pains –
dusty whirrings, last things,

a house of windowless rooms.

Cap Stone
Mark 12: 10

If you were to tell me, now, as the foxes emerge from their improvised dwellings,
as night emerges with inestimable patience from under improvised day,
to – step *down* from this, desist, unmake what is made and forbear from making
what is not yet made I would rise like oxygen in water, I would rise through all
space and hold my face up to the moon as to a looking glass.
Tell me I am not with the real and this voice is not in the grain of life and I
will take, this instant, a nebula in my left palm and melt the deep
cold of its cancelled fire merely with the heat of my hand,
drinking all distance, making my body the chorus of time.
And the very stones of my eyes would cry out, then, against
you, and my flint tongue would strike sparks – off pinnacle, cap stone, firmament

To the Reader

Am I telling the thought?
Am I telling the thought like a truth?
Am I telling the truth like an attempt on the truth?
Is the attempt bloody enough for you yet? For me?

(O, of dust and spittle,
the metals of blood,

is this and this – all this!

of dust
and the mettle of blood.)

Trieste

Our thin futon mattress on loose parquet,
white sheets, the sanctus of our skin.
Then light wakes me early.

                A coolness, doves.

Morning comes like a proof,
grief-balancing two hearts, where what's
between them is held like the bubble in a spirit level.

Crooked, violable is the way of the angel,

                a candescent road.

Later we'll lark in the tideless winter sea
then turn our faces back to the sky to find it
carbon, dark as the lord of hosts.

                All those sceptres of lightning.

Here, a few miles down the coast from Duino,
Rilke's shade still asks the sea wind
'What is coming? What approaches?'

And weather, like a Spartan messenger,

                runs in, breathless